Le

Divina

Spiritual Reading of the Bible

by Jean Khoury

All booklets are published thanks to the
generous support of the members of the
Catholic Truth Society

CATHOLIC TRUTH SOCIETY
PUBLISHERS TO THE HOLY SEE

Contents

Jean Khoury BSc MA received his Theology degrees from the *Teresianum* in Rome and from the *Institut Catholique* of Toulouse. He is a highly respected authority for his work on spiritual life and an international author of several books on spirituality and meditation, as well as many articles and studies on mysticism. Jean lectures and leads retreats worldwide on spiritual life and meditation. He also practices Spiritual Counselling in London.

Preface

Lectio divina is an ancient Latin expression which means 'spiritual reading of the Bible'. It includes a wide scale of activities which can lead us from a mere reading of the Bible to a high contemplation and it is regarded as a treasure of the Christian faith.

This book focuses for the first time on a unique method of listening to God every day, through the daily readings of the Bible. It is a method which brings about a real change in our life and powerfully nourishes our personal relationship with Jesus.

Although many Christians read and meditate on the daily readings, only the classical way of 'reading-meditating-contemplating' has ever been presented. This book revolutionises the method as it brings a greater clarity on the subject and proposes a simple but efficient way to listen to God daily. It makes the action of God accessible to everyone and shows that our dialogue with God can be very real. So from the image we may have of a 'silent-distant-mysterious God', we are led to a new experience where he speaks to us every day, follows us and transforms our lives.

Even if this book was primarily written for a Catholic audience, it can be read by any Christian who wants to listen to Jesus daily through the Bible, with the help of his Holy Spirit. Many churches propose two readings daily, and here we explain how to take advantage of this immense gift given to us by God in his Word.

Jean Khoury
London, February 2002

The Basics of *Lectio*

Introduction

The eternal and uncreated Word became human words to nourish us with his divine life. Like a beautiful stained glass window, the words of the Bible let the light of God shine through and illuminate us.

The Bible is like a sacrament; a visible sign of an invisible grace, it has a human aspect, the words and the divine life within it. The sacramental reality of the Bible tells us that through its words we are able:

1. *to receive God himself*
God is an uncreated being, which is beyond the grasp of our understanding. Through the human words of the Bible we are able to receive his divine life.

2. *to understand his words through our senses and intellect*
We use our senses, vision and hearing to grasp the human meaning of the words we read, and our intellect and will work together to gain the necessary understanding of a text.

3. *to be nourished by his words in our hearts*

The words of the Bible carry a divine life which nourishes primarily our heart or spirit. The words transcend our senses and intellect to reach this highest region of our being and transform it into God himself.

Without being aware of it, we may have a sterile attitude in the face of a text. The aim of the text is to transform us: however, we may remain at a level of reception that seems to nurture our intellect but does not lead to true conversion. The Word then does not attain its goal because of our distorted approach: we are no longer receiving a Sacrament but looking at a text. And, considering only the text, we are no longer in touch with the uncreated incarnate Word, Jesus. Instead of listening, we stay on the level of a good explanation of the text or, even worse, that of simply projecting our own subjective feelings - i.e. our problems and desires - onto it. If Scripture is to nurture us, in both soul and spirit, we must be determined to let ourselves be disturbed, converted, jostled and enlightened by what we read, instead of looking for what may comfort us.

There is a big difference between, on the one hand 'understanding' the Word of God and, on the other hand, 'knowing' it. Understanding the Word leads to what Saint Paul said: I know what I should do, but I do not do it; the Word is unable to become incarnate in my acts and in my life (cf. *Rm* 7:18 and *Ga* 5:17).

Conversely, we can say we truly know the Word when, through an authentic and miraculous daily conversion, it really is incarnated in our lives. This is 'miraculous' because it is an operation that touches the will and heals it. The will truly is ill in the sense that there exists a chasm between our intellect and our will we know what we should do, but the will does not follow through. Saint Paul noted this when he said: I do not do what I think is right.

When approaching the Bible, two levels must be distinguished:

1 - the level of understanding
2 - the level of listening

In order to understand a text, one must make use of all the tools the intellect has to offer, including diverse methods of exegesis. However, this is far from a true *lectio divina*; we need to listen to what the Lord says to us through the text. The first step leads us to understand the meaning(s) of the text. In the second step, its task is to be the instrument of the one who wants to speak to me today and nurture me. The text is destined to become a

Sacrament. The Uncreated Word became flesh; it became a human word, not in the sense of being diminished or diluted, but in the sense that the Uncreated Word used the human word as a Sacrament to come to us and bond himself to us. We can analyse the material dimension of this sacrament (the literal, created human aspect of the text), but this will never give us God! It will give us an understanding of the text, a widening of the icon which constitutes its material dimension, but it will not give us the Uncreated Light. Both levels need to be maintained simultaneously. The aim is not to submit to what is irrational but to 'sacramentalise' what is rational, to make it transparent so that the Uncreated Light may come through. Although we can make an excellent and intelligent analysis of a text, we are called to do something quite different. We have not yet gone into the process of simple *lectio!*

We can base all of *lectio* and its necessity on the words of the Lord: "apart from me you are not able to do anything" (*Jn* 15:5) and on the inner attitude of the Son of Man described in John 5:19a-20: "Verily, verily, I say to you, The Son is not able to do anything of himself, if he does not see the Father doing it; for whatever He does, these things the Son also does in a like manner; for the Father loves the Son, and **shows** him all that he himself is doing." These words are said in reference to the Son of Man, and consequently they refer to all men.

We must "see the Father doing"; *lectio* allows this. The essential point is for us to introduce all our conscious activity into this movement, to slowly submit it to God's influence and to his action. This is the very basis of Christian life and of *lectio*. If we do not do this, we are simply self-constructing our own personal being, our activities, our daily programme, our Christianity, and doing so in vain (*Ps* 127:1). We should meditate for a long time on the seriousness of Christ's words: "apart from me you are not able to do anything". And, as a consequence: "I will show you my will each day and will give you what you need for putting it into practice." Anyone wanting to build Christian life or prayer life without these foundations is fooling himself, he is running away and straying.

Christ's central place in this process

Christ, the only mediator between God and man

When we are doing *lectio*, that is to say when we open ourselves to listen to God, we are facing Christ. Christ is the Word the Father has given to us, his only word, and he asks us to listen to himself attentively. Christ, who is both God and man, is the only mediator between God and us. We will see further on that the process of *lectio* is a process of incarnation. But it is the incarnation of the Word of God in us, the incarnation of Christ in us. We will never let Christ out of our sight: he is essential.

Christ reveals the Father

Christ is at the heart of the Gospel. In St John he is presented with the specific function of revealing God the Father. "No one has ever seen God; the Son alone has made him known" (*Jn* 1:18). The Son allows us to hear the Father's voice, and to see his appearance *eidos* (*Jn* 5:37-38). By sounding the Scriptures, we are led to the Son who is the Word of the Father and he gives us eternal life (cf. *Jn* 5:19-47).

Christ at the heart of spiritual life

This is the fundamental point of all spiritual life. Saint Teresa of Jesus asked herself for a long time whether, in perfect contemplation, one continued to consider Christ in his humanity, or whether it was better to be attentive to the vastness of God's divinity. The answer given by the theologians of her time was in conformity with the Gospel and Saint Paul: the fullness of the divinity lives in him, in bodily form (cf. *Col* 2:9) and we find hidden in him all the treasures of Wisdom and Knowledge (cf. *Col* 2:3). Saint John of the Cross, just like Saint Teresa of Jesus, invites us to contemplate the humanity of the Son with the eyes of the Father: "For, in giving us, as He did, His Son, which is His Word - and He has no other - He spoke to us all together, once and for all, in this single Word, and He has no occasion

10

to speak further". To Him we must listen; and He is the one we encounter and listen to through *lectio*.

The primary impulse of lectio

The primary impulse of *lectio* is to introduce us into a relationship of divine friendship with the Lord, to allow him to speak to us and to (progressively) tell us all things: "No longer do I call you servants, for the servant does not know what his lord does. But I have called you **friends**, for everything that I heard from my Father, I have made known to you" (*Jn* 15:15). Telling everything to another person truly is a sign of love. "...the Father loves the Son, and shows to him all that he himself is doing" (*Jn* 5:20a). *Lectio* is the eminent place where Christ-God will be able to speak to us, today, and tell what he wants us to do. He will explain it to us: "and beginning from Moses, and from all the prophets, he explained to them in all the Scriptures the things about himself" (*Lk* 24:27).

It is impossible to assert that one should live by blind faith alone, opposing it to the understanding we get from the Word of God. Faith finds its sustenance in God's Word. If this Word is absent, faith becomes very meagre. Conversely, the Word of God, above all else, can fortify it. Faith is, firstly, the belief in a word that has been given. God speaks every day, he wants to speak to us: that is the basis of our faith. He will not

11

say anything to us other than his Son, his Word, that he will give to us by little mouthfuls, in packages of light. We have a right, that of listening each day to the Lord who speaks to us and guides us. He wants his Word to remain in us; on this condition alone can we bear fruit that will remain for eternal life, "if you remain in me, and my words in you may remain, you may ask whatever you wish, and it shall be done to you. In this way my Father will be glorified, that you will bear much fruit, and you shall become my disciples" (*Jn* 15:7-8). We need to maintain a living and daily contact with the Word so that it may be active in our lives. People (and I am thinking particularly of those consecrated to God) who do not frequent the Word of God assiduously and on a daily basis let their faith and their dynamism die down, and easily slip away toward a human project and human thoughts. Their joy of living for God and of giving themselves to him, recedes before a lifestyle, which may be very active but where there is no place for God: it is without sap and without light. One's faith is directly proportional to one's contact with the Word of God. As the Psalm says: "Those who look to Yahweh, are radiant" (*Ps* 34:5). Looking to God means seeing His face; now, His face is His Son, the Son who speaks in the Scriptures; His face can only be seen surely in the Scriptures. This is how the life of God shines forth. Listening to God implies becoming familiar with his way of thinking, getting used to thinking like him, seeing things as he does.

The immense importance of *lectio*

Lectio is extremely important for spiritual life. It brings us to realise the deep mystery of our vocation: the incarnation of Christ in our life, in our entire being. We are beings who have been given an intellect, a will and freedom. These faculties of the soul must be transformed into Christ; he must live there, but until that is realised, they are ill, and each one needs to be healed in its particular way. Through the contact *lectio* establishes between the supernatural and each of these conscious and active faculties, it opens the way to a genuine transformation of our being. Of course, it is inseparable from *mental prayer*, which works on the deeper levels of our being, but it is indispensable. We feed our faculties every day with the daily events of our lives and we are not conscious of the fact that this food is often different, when not in actual opposition, to God's thought and will. *Lectio*, on the other hand, is a path leading straight to conversion. It accomplishes a daily miracle, the sole miracle Christ wishes to accomplish in us.

Basic activity of the Fathers, the common monastic practice

Is the practice of *lectio* something new? No, all the monks and all the Church Fathers practiced this way of meditating on the Word of God, and even today it is still common practice among monks. However, it is not exclusively reserved to them; the monk is the one who, being a beacon and a light for the Church, gives the example of conversion and of the best way to achieve it. The Church Fathers were accustomed to the Scriptures, they all read, meditated and explained them. Through the Scriptures they could contemplate God. The Catechism of the Catholic Church reminds us of this: "Seek in **reading** and you will find in **meditating**; knock in *mental prayer* and it will be opened to you by **contemplation**" (CCC 2654). Furthermore, it may be noted that most of the Church Fathers started out as monks.

Listening, discovering God's will, its fulfillment

The aim of *lectio,* as we are presenting it here, is to listen to Christ, to receive a living and active word every day. This implies discerning the newness that is characteristic of a way of listening that leads to transformation. We can thus discover God's will each day. We are pushed to put this word into practice and, in this way, to sanctify ourselves, to really transform ourselves. What is intended is the incarnation of the Word that God wants to speak to us today; this is like a little Annunciation.

The Readings of the Mass
(a particular grace of Vatican II)

The Second Vatican Council allowed the Church to realise anew the place of the table of the Word of God in the celebration of Mass. With the distribution of Scripture throughout the liturgical years, the Church permitted God's people to be nourished more abundantly. Generally, the liturgy offers two readings, regardless of the Rites. In *lectio*, it is preferable to stay with these readings so as to eliminate our own human interference, as much as possible, from the listening process. The Church has already chosen the texts and so we receive them as coming from God - in the Rite of our choice. If we choose texts ourselves, we introduce a factor of personal preference that defiles the listening process. Opening the Bible 'at random' is neither a satisfying nor a lasting solution. This is especially true because, when we do this, we are expecting to find an answer to a particular problem. Now, as we will see, we must not impose on the Lord the point he wants to discuss with us today.

The Process of *Lectio*

Morning solitude

We need to begin the process of *lectio* in a quiet place of solitude. "But you, when you pray, go into your room, close your door, and pray to your Father who is there in secret" (*Mt* 6:6). The morning is the best time for this because the mind is freer and more vigorous, and the light received will be of use all throughout the day. "And very early, before the beginning of the day, having risen, he went out to a deserted place, and there he prayed" (*Mk* 1:35). Certain people read before they go to bed, and that is good, they consider that the Word works while they sleep (cf. *Mk* 4:26-29), and this is true. However, it is insufficient; when we want to meet someone we do not encounter that person in our sleep. Now, the Lord wishes to speak to us, he has something to say to our waking mind, and wants to enlighten and guide it throughout the day. For these reasons it is good and even preferable to do *lectio* early in the morning. In any case, it would be useless to do it when one is tired. Our attention is important, because *lectio* is an exercise that requires the use of all one's existential energy and therefore, when tired, we are not in the best state for it. Doing it under these conditions would simply not be serious; it would be better to get some rest.

Before Christ

So we are facing Christ and not just a text; and we want to listen to him. He wants to speak to us through the Readings of the Mass. We usually have two texts: an Epistle (or a passage of the Old Testament [in the Latin Rite]) and the Gospel. The references can be found in any liturgical calendar. The aim is not to analyse the texts, nor to study them. Reading the Bible, studying, going to Bible-study classes, reading the commentaries of the Fathers, all of this is useful and does not conflict with *lectio*, but these things should be done at another time: they are simply not the same activity as *lectio*. We may say to ourselves: "Now, I will listen to the Lord who wants to speak to me" but, if I have already meditated on the same text previously, the Lord will be able to tell me something 'new' today. The process of *lectio* requires me to make an act of faith: "these two texts are God's words and, therefore, the Word of God". The same texts may say different things to different people and to the same, at a different moment in his spiritual journey. The Word of God accompanies the believer and gives him what he needs according to the spiritual state he is in. We must believe this. Let's take an example: A man taking part in an Ignatian retreat was to meditate on the texts. He already knew one of the texts as he had meditated on it before, so he left it aside. When the Priest accompanying him found out about this, he sent him back to his room to take up the 'well-known' text again and listen to what the Lord had to say to him. He was truly surprised to discover that this text spoke 'differently', that is, in a new way; but it is possible that the words now striking him were not the same ones he had noted the first time. Each time it is as if the Lord were marking a different word or phrase of the text with a highlighter!

Reading the two texts

The first request; re-reading

We begin by invoking the Holy Spirit. A possible prayer would be: 'Come, Holy Spirit, illuminate me, help me to understand the Word today'. After invoking Him, we read through the text, it is normal to understand the contents of the text; but this effort to understand should not be transformed into exegetical research or deep study. The notes at the bottom of the page may be used, but without being dwelt on.

Let us then ask the Lord to tell us what He wants: "Speak, Lord, your servant is listening." This is the first request and the most important one because the entire evolution of the process of lectio depends on it.

The quality of the request; the example of the blind man

The quality of this request is decisive. It should be made with a pure intention, with all the energy of our being. The best illustration of the quality necessary for this first request is the call of the blind man who had probably heard one of his beggar friends from another village talk about the Lord who had healed him. One day, while he is sitting on the roadside, he hears the commotion of a crowd. He asks what's happening, and someone tells him that Jesus of Nazareth, in Galilee, is going by. He remembers his friend who has been healed and now sees. His hope is roused, and he cries out: "Son of David, have mercy on me!" The crowd continues to pass, he cries out again, "Son of David, have mercy on me!" People push him away from the road; he is a nuisance. The disciples tell him to pipe down and not to disturb the Master, but the blind man just keeps getting louder, because the Lord does not seem to be paying attention to him. Then the Lord turns around and asks him to be brought forward. "The blind man throws off his cloak and jumping up onto his feet runs toward Jesus". - What do you want? - I want to see. - Do you believe that I can heal you? - Yes. - May this happen on account of your faith. And immediately he was healed.

When this man asked the Lord to give him his sight back, he was not just passing time, amusing himself or asking out of intellectual curiosity. **His entire being was calling out to be healed** and to see. He knew what he was expecting the Lord to do, he knew that he could heal him. We should have this same attitude; a request coming from our entire being, as if it was a matter of life or death, a desire to be healed, the desire to see, to see something more for today. And when we go to the doctor we are not ashamed of showing our wounds. In the same way, here we leave him free; we present him our entire being and ask him to act as he wills.

The first reading is not enough
After reading the text for a first time, we may retain a word or a sentence of the text that speaks to us more than the rest. It is therefore possible that the Lord is using this word or sentence to say something to us, but we are not entirely certain of this. The rest of the work aims at acquiring the certainty that this is truly what he wants of us. We usually have a tendency - the majority of the time - to project our own thoughts into

the text. In fact, we come with our problems and impose them onto the Lord, asking him to throw light on them and to give us a solution. He knows very well what we need, he knows our problems, but often, he wants to deal with something else, with something simpler and more concrete. We, on the other hand only want to talk about what troubles us! We need to know how to let go and, from the very beginning of the *lectio*, entrust our problems to him. Actually by putting them on his shoulders, we are doing exactly what we need to in order to be able to listen. A psalm reminds us of this: "Unload your burden on Yahweh and he will sustain you" (*Ps* 55:22); and the Lord himself says: "Come to me, all you who labour and are burdened, and I will give you rest" (*Mt* 11:28). He cares for all our worries.

In the parable of the sower, the third patch of ground is good soil but it is covered with thorns. Now, these thorns do not represent our problems, because always there are some, but rather they suggest worry, which restrains our hearts like a rope or a heavy chain. "[Other seeds] fell in among the thorns, and the thorns rose up and choked them" (*Mt* 13:7). "And that sown among the thorns, is the one who hears the word, and the **anxiety** of this age, and the **seduction** of the riches, choke the word, and it becomes unfruitful" (*Mt* 13:22).

Like a stone on the bottom of the sea, we are paralysed by worry, as if worry were able to change things. "And who of you, by worrying, is able to add one cubit to his life?" (*Mt* 6:27); "you are not able to make one hair white or black" (*Mt* 5:36). Now, these chains stifle the Word and prevent us from listening to what the Lord wants to say to us. We must therefore hand over to the Lord everything that preoccupies us. By freeing our heart in this way, we can consecrate ourselves to the 'one thing that is needed': the quest for the Kingdom.

The Lord tells us: "Seek first the kingdom of God and other things will be given to you as well" (*Mt* 6:33). But, in fact, in the majority of our situations, we reverse the Lord's advice and we ask for the "other things" and, if there's a small place left, we put "the kingdom of God" at the end of our list. But this is precisely what the Gentiles do, in the words of the Lord, as if a man's life depended on his immediate needs. We forget that he is aware of all our needs and looks after them, and that we should not ask for perishable things. He does invite us insistently to "Ask and you shall receive"; in fact, he tells us to ask for the Holy Spirit, the will of God. In thus giving the first place to God, the heart purifies itself, since the purity of the heart consists in giving this first place to God in a genuine and concrete way.

It usually happens that, even after the first reading of the text, we do not find today's divine light. This may be so either because the text is difficult or because we lack concentration. It then needs to be re-read a second or third time or even more.

Not just ideas

The aim is not to pick ideas out of the text. Once someone asking himself if he had done his *lectio* well made a list of the ideas he had found: there were 12 in the first text and 5 in the second, so altogether 17. However, in reality we should come up with: 1 + 1 = 1, since Christ speaks a single word to us through both texts. We should avoid applying our intellect to the text, as this would be a mistake. We need to be receptive, and that is the most difficult thing to be. Our intellect should not only be silenced but also 'malleable' before the text, just like a light-sensitive film, while we wait for a word, a sentence to speak out to us, to imprint itself upon us and come to life, more luminous and more intense than the remainder of the text.

Rules of discernment: am I listening or not?

Two texts, one word (95%)

Even after several readings of the first text, sometimes we may not find anything. (The order of reading is not absolute, and one can begin with the Gospel.) Then we go on to the second text, and read it attentively. In general, with the Gospel, things light up more easily.

However, it could also happen that we receive several beams of light and not just one. We do not know which one comes from the Lord. This brings out the interest of having two texts. Like two lines that can only cross one another at a single point, two texts can only touch on a single idea, 'for me', today. One text filters the other, and each text eliminates the elements that ought not remain in the other. On the following diagram the short lines on each long line represent the succession of ideas in each text.

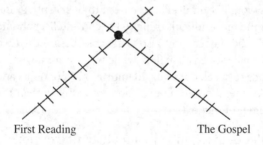

First Reading   The Gospel

At the end, we notice that the Lord only says one thing at a time through the two texts. There is no need to search for words that are literally the same, for example 'mercy' here and 'merciful' there. Generally, the two texts are not connected, the first one may be an extract from one of St Paul's epistles, and the second from the Gospel of St Matthew. Each author follows his own direction. The only common denominator of the two texts is that both are the Word of God and if we encounter the same idea in one and the other, this is either a mere coincidence, or we are starting to hear the Lord.

The fact that the Lord speaks to us through these two texts, with one single idea, brings our certainty to '95%' that he actually has spoken and this does not come from us or from our desires. This is **the main criterion** to be taken into account and verified. And, although we are going to give four other criteria, we should base ourselves primarily on this one because it guarantees the highest degree of certainty. Indeed, this criterion is itself the channel through which the light comes. It lets us mark out the light. Given its course (from God, through the texts, to one person) and given the fact that it is divine, this light is not multiple but 'one.' Until we have only one single idea, **one** light beam, we must continue beckoning God by asking for his Holy Spirit and the revelation of his will for us today.

In the following paragraphs we will discuss the four complementary signs that help us confirm the origin of the received light. Even if the explanation is longer, these four signs in terms of importance only constitute '5%' of the weight! This must not be forgotten in the discernment process.

Let us now consider the four signs that allow us to complete this certainty that a given word actually does come from the Lord.

The four signs

The single word received has at least four characteristics. Before dealing with them, let us see what composes a human being. In the following diagram we see the two zones of our being: the intellect and the will.

We will better understand what the intellect and the will are if we note the words of Saint Paul: "you do not do what you would like to do" (*Ga* 5:17). So, I have within me volition, i.e. the thought, the intellect, which recognizes the good thing to do, and then the agent of my activities, i.e. the will, the acts. Saint Paul remarks that, in him, and in each of us, there is a break between the intellect that knows what is good and the will that does not accomplish it.

The diagram clearly shows this break. It is a gap in us separating the two faculties of the soul: the intellect and the will. We also note that the will is ill since it cannot accomplish what the intellect discerns. The weakness and illness of the will are shown by the grey covering the zone that indicates it. The number (1) on the diagram represents the call of the blind man who wants to see; while God's answer is symbolised by the arrow coming from above and touching the will at a concrete point, an area in our life which needs to be changed or where something needs to be done. In the diagram the area of the will in need of healing is darker than the rest of the zone of the will. This arrow pointing from above symbolises the light received.

Let us now analyse the four most important characteristics of this arrow, which help corroborate our discernment.

A new taste

An example will help us to better grasp the characteristics and action of this light (symbolised by the descending arrow). 'The other day we had a dispute with someone and he was rude and spoke badly of us, or even did us harm and hurt us. Our heart is filled with bitterness. At best, we do not hate this person but we do not want to hear anything about him'. And just today, as if by chance (but, of course, there is no 'by chance' with the Lord), during the process of *lectio*, the Lord gives us this word to hear: 'Go reconcile yourself with that person, pray for him, bless him'. This word is a new light beam that penetrates our intellect. It suggests a concrete action, and we understand that it comes from God and not from us. By penetrating us, this light received gives our intellect an impression of newness. This is confirmed by the fact that the indication God gives us is really the last thing we would have liked to hear today. Our usual inclination ('the old us') would have preferred something else, but the Lord highlights some aspect he wants to change in us, to transform within us. We feel the contrast between this new light and our usual state. This first characteristic, 'the new taste', results from an 'intrusion' of the Holy Spirit. Or, in other words, even if the comparison is too strong, it is like the apparition of the Lord to the Apostles locked in the upper room - He suddenly appears.

When *lectio* is practiced on a daily basis, a new desire arises in us, an expectation of the hour when we will meet the Lord and when something will be 'revealed' to us. We can compare this spiritual desire with the human desire we have to listen to the latest news, to read the paper or when waiting for a letter from a dear friend or waiting to meet him. *Lectio* is really never boring. All these aspects together are the basis on which the first characteristic defines itself: the word has a taste of newness because it comes from God.

Practicality

The second characteristic is this, we notice that the given word is concrete, that it touches the ill part of our will. It is not some word addressed to our neighbours; we are not doing their meditation. Nor is it a theoretical meditation on some point of the Christian faith. No, this word concerns something concrete, calling for a particular act or action from us, a real change of the will. The arrow illustrates this, its point touches our will, indeed it will be a particular area of our will where a change or transformation is necessary. We must therefore have a true desire for conversion, each time, so that the light may penetrate right down to our will. Otherwise, refusal and flight will prevent the light from descending and reaching the will. Not that it does not have this aim, but we hinder it from achieving its goal. This shows us how essential the quality of our attitude is. The Lord unceasingly says to us: "I stand at the door, and I knock"; I won't force you, I don't impose myself on my friends' freedom! They have to decide to open the door. This is the fundamental know-how of prayer (whether of *lectio* or *mental prayer*, each according to its own methods). If one does not want to be healed, or even worse, if someone thinks that he does not need healing, it is useless for that person to approach Christ or his word.

So we see that this word, which Christ speaks to us, is concrete; it touches the will and incites us to a particular action. This action may be simultaneously inward and exterior, as in our example: 'reconcile yourself with your neighbour.' However, it may also be only an inward action which is necessary, for example an act of detachment, of confidence or a sacrifice. No one sees it, but it may cost us great effort.

So the second characteristic of the light received in *lectio* is its concrete facet, which leads to true change, to conversion.

A word that seems of 'little' value

We might consider that the word He speaks to us is very 'little'. What does 'little' mean? In our life, through the contemplation of the cross, we came to understand that the Lord united himself to each of us in a unique way. Therefore, the cross is not firstly an instrument for torture or a place of suffering; it is rather the place of our union with Christ, the clear and irrevocable promise of our union with Him. This union, the fruit he obtained for us by His death on the cross, is called to slowly be accomplished, day after day. In fact, we are looking at the summit of Mount thabor and wishing we were already there. The child within us wants everything immediately, and finds little indication in the Lord's words to him that would permit arriving there quickly. We are disappointed and we do not understand, or we could put it this way: the Lord wants us to be living fully, here and now, and we are disconcerted by his silence concerning the things that we believe to be important or essential and that, in reality, do not attract his attention. We do not see why the Lord gives so much attention to tiny little things. A married man might one day be asked to put his napkin on the table differently because, for the past twenty years, he has been placing it in a way that irritates his wife. And the Lord actually comes and asks him to do that! It is strange how such a little thing is given such great importance

31

when there is a big project to be realised: one's union with God, or at a time when so many people are dying from hunger or AIDS. This is so because Christian life is made of little things and of faithfulness in little things: "Well done, good and faithful servant, you have been faithful over a few things, I will set you over many things" (*Mt* 25:21). Life on earth consists of this faithfulness in little things whilst we, on the contrary, are looking at the top of the mountain. It is good to look on high, to dream and dream well, St Teresa of Jesus recommends this. She asks her daughters to have elevated thoughts and great desires; but we need to keep our eyes on the little step in front of us, the step that contains within itself the entire mountain for today, for without it we could not reach the summit. That is the realism of the Gospel. What use is it really to think about tomorrow and to wait for tomorrow's directives, if we do not do today's work? "Each day has enough problems of its own" (*Mt* 6:34).

Impossibility

Although this word appears trivial to us, it will seem impossible for us to put into practice. 'I am incapable of going and reconciling myself with the person who hurt me because my heart is full of bitterness and paralysed. What should I do? I do know that this is the will of God, but I just cannot do it.'

32

One day a young rich man came to see the Lord, at this point one might object that, as we are not rich therefore this Gospel passage does not apply to us. However if we look a little closer, we will find that we can be richer through our desires. Even if I am materially poor, I may wish to own a nice car or to have a good job. Therefore, I am still caught up in the possessions of my desires! It is impossible to fool the Lord, we are all rich. In that sense, this Gospel passage is addressed to all of us.

So it is a good thing to enter into the role of the young man by applying this text to ourselves and to ask, with him, for eternal life or, more simply, to follow the Lord and to be united to him. This is the goal of Christian life, and the love of the Lord on the cross reveals it to us. He died in order to unite us with him. This union is not, as some think, reserved to monks and religious, or to so called 'born saints'. No, Christ died for everyone and for each one of us, for you in a special way; and you therefore have the vocation to be united to him. We must use all the possibilities he gives to us to receive all that he obtained for us on the cross.

Here we are then with the young rich man who wants eternal life. The Lord asks him: "Have you observed the commandments?" And he replies that he has, since his childhood. The Lord looks at him and says to him: "You only lack one thing, go, sell all your possessions, give the price to the poor, and then come and follow me". The Gospel tells us: "The young man, having heard the word, went away sorrowful, for he had many possessions". This is the feeling we have when the Lord wants us to abandon something we are attached to, or to do something we are not used to doing. We are so deeply stuck in our habits that they have become a part of us, and when the Lord tugs at it, it is as if he were trying to tear off a part of ourselves. Then, "Jesus said to his disciples, 'Verily I say to you, it is difficult for a rich man to enter into the Kingdom of the heavens'" (*Mt* 19:23). And the Lord goes even further and insists: "again I say to you, it is easier for a camel to go through the eye of a needle, than for a rich man to enter into the Kingdom of God". In short, it is impossible.

To put the Gospel into practice, it is necessary to make an effort: "Strive to go in through the straight gate" (*Lk* 13:24), "for many are called, and few chosen" (*Mt* 22:14). But there is a great danger in this, for one might be misled into reducing life in Christ to a matter of volition. The Lord assuredly shows us in this passage that this is not the case. We do not accomplish our Christian vocation through the force of our will but rather through the humility of our entreaty. We also encounter this impossibility of accomplishing the commandments of

God, according to the light of the Gospel, in the Sermon on the Mount. Here the Lord quotes the commandments God gave to Moses on Mount Sinai, with the introduction, "You heard that it was said", and then he puts them under the light of the Gospel, "but I say to you". And, in this, we see that he wants us to fulfill the commandments deeply and radically; and, at this point, we realise that it is simply 'too much' whoever gets angry against his brother shall be in danger of the Gehenna of the fire! And a man should not desire a woman in his heart because, in reality, according to God, he has already committed adultery with her in his heart! "Who can be saved"? The disciples let all of the Gospel's light enter into their hearts, it penetrated them from head to foot but they show that they are honest, "And his disciples having heard, were amazed, saying, 'Who, then, is able to be saved?'" (*Mt* 19:25). In fact, someone might be able to leave everything, be detached from his parents, even his children, his wife, but renouncing oneself is quite another matter! It is perhaps at the moment a person discovers his radical inability to follow Christ that he truly becomes a Christian for the first time! Saint Paul did assert, "Though the will to do what is good is in me, the strength to do it is not" (*Rm* 7:18).

Wishing is not doing. 'I wish to do the will of God but am incapable of accomplishing it'. We must therefore go beyond our inability. It is our normal condition, but on the other hand, it is necessary to transform it into a prayer, "Lord, since this is what you're asking of me and you want me to accomplish it, you can do so by giving me the necessary strength. Therefore, give me this strength, your Holy Spirit, so that the word you want me to put into practice may become incarnate in my life today". Saint Augustine says this in his own way: "Lord, help me to do what you command and command what you will". He asks for the strength of God (this is our second request) in order to be able to accomplish what God asks; and then he leaves the Lord free to ask whatever he wills.

When we feel difficulty in what God is asking of us, or when our will refuses to act, this indicates that the 'old us' is still there - although we do understand why God is suggesting this action. Indeed, his request is in purposeful contradiction with our 'old will', and the Lord wants to heal it. This repulsion and feelings of impossibility are consequently normal. He did say to Peter that his ways are disconcerting: "another will gird you, and take you where you do not want to go" (Jn 21:18).

We clearly realise how and in what sense this word seems impossible to us and at this point it is important to remember that we need the assistance of God to enact the 'impossible'.

In the previous paragraphs, we analysed the first request and the light that comes out of it. We saw the main way to discern if the light perceived is really the light of God - as described previously. We also had further clarification by verifying the light received through the four signs. Now we will sum up the whole process of the *lectio* including the second and final request.

The process of *lectio*; two requests

Lectio includes only two requests that bring two respective answers from God. The first request (1) (see diagram below) is: "Lord tell me what you want of me" or "let me see the step to take today". And the second (2) is: "Lord, give me your Holy Spirit **in order to** incarnate and **realise** what you are asking of me".

The second request has as its main goal to receive the help of the Holy Spirit to realise what he asked us to do in his first answer. It is obvious that without his strength 'impossibility' remains impossible. Following the second request the Lord replies, giving us his strength to act; the received impulsion helps us fulfill what he has asked. He will heal our heart and give it the strength to pray for the person who has offended us, to go and pardon him. The response of grace is represented, in the diagram (b), by the arrow penetrating and transforming the will.

Lectio is in fact only accomplished when, in receiving his power, our will is transformed and becomes able to **realise** his light; the divine union of heaven and earth.

Attention should be paid to the fact that the second arrow goes beyond the gap separating the intellect from the will and touches the area or the point in question. Conversely, the first descending arrow, indicating the point the Lord wants to heal, does not yet touch the will. It shows and indicates but does not yet act. The Lord always has the extraordinary delicacy of never (or, at least almost never) pushing us.

Getting *Lectio* Right

The following paragraphs are meant to shed more light on the process of *lectio* and to help us to live and appreciate it more.

Lectio is completed through life; its benefits

As we know, the second request of the *lectio* is: "Lord give me your Holy Spirit in order to realise what you asked me". However the *lectio* does not end there! We need, with the help of the Holy Spirit, to put into practice the light we received. Only then the *lectio* is realised and accomplished. It is by going and reconciling ourselves with the person indicated by God that the 'course' of his Word will have been completed. This Word ("go and reconcile yourself with your brother"), which came down from the highest heaven, spoken in the heart of the Trinity, touches the densest part of our being, our body (through the concrete act of reconciliation). This is the course of the word. It unites heaven and earth. It is always necessary to ensure that the Word received, like a beam of light coming from the mouth of God, is truly incarnated. Otherwise *lectio* will remain fruitless. Conversely, if the word is incarnated we will notice remarkable progress and are certain to see changes rapidly occurring in our life:

- it is more ordered

- greater clarity of the ideas and the acts accomplished all throughout the day

- a stronger faith

- a will that frees itself from slavery, and becomes more solid, firmer in the will of God

- consolation and strength coming from the daily encounter with the living Christ and hearing him who speaks to us in our attentive silence and guides us in what to do

- finally, staunch perseverance and resistance in life's trials.

In addition to this, it is good to note that one of the greatest advantages of *lectio* is simply the fact that our intellect is no longer at the mercy of the many thoughts jostling it; it has become disciplined, since it is nurtured by an intense light which illuminates it from the morning on and all throughout the day. A man's thoughts are a major source of his suffering. *Lectio*, by reforming the intellect, educates it and protects it against worry provoked by thoughts, because it transforms and replaces them through the light received. Instead of being haunted by worries, thoughts and the trouble they engender, our intellect is unified around the light received; this peace of mind is of great value.

"Lord, I have done, through your grace, what you asked me to do this morning"

At the end of the day, by revising our acts, we can see if we have achieved what he, in the morning, asked us to do through the *lectio*. We will be able to say: "Lord, I have done, with your help, what you asked me to do this morning". It is a great satisfaction to find that we have been able, with the help of God, to achieve a 'spiritual' step. Firmly accomplishing day after day what he asks us to do allows the Lord to hold us, and so he may pull us closer to him as the days go by. This will help us to keep our joys focused on the purest goals. Our happiness will be centred on fulfilling the will of God. In fact we won't try to look for any other joys, even if we have many imperfections and failures.

At the beginning we might find it hard to practice *lectio* for 55 minutes

People are usually surprised to learn that it is necessary to dedicate 55 minutes to this listening exercise and practice of the word: "Why does it take so much time?" "We are not pure spirits!" It takes time for the light to pass through the spirit to the soul, i.e. from the most secret part where God communicates himself to us (the spirit or heart in the biblical sense), to the conscious and awakened part of our being (the soul: the active intellect and will). Because of its weight, the body slows down this operation, it takes time to perceive and to become conscious. Patience and perseverance are necessary. Moreover, the light received may appear a bit hazy at first, so one must repeat the request and insist until the word becomes clear and intelligible, until it makes sense to us, and this takes time. So why do we need to insist until the word becomes clear? Precisely because we have the right to an intelligible word, given that we are beings endowed with reason and need it in order to act. Would the one who gave us his blood, who died for us so that we might be saved, refuse us a daily word when he prescribed us to ask for it every day: "Give us today our daily bread"? He cannot refuse to give the word that can save us, a word indicating what is to be done each day. He asks us to apply our will in doing his will: "Thy will be done on earth as in heaven": how then could he deprive us of this knowledge, which is so important for our salvation?! He wants to treat us like friends and not like servants; and everything is said to a friend, nothing is hidden from him (*Jn* 14:21).

As one experiences this authentic and daily supernatural action, one experiences the strength and power of God's light, and this will lead to the desire to spend well beyond the fixed time, up to 75 minutes. At this point an indication needs to be given, since it is clear that one feels the need to stay longer. We need to know what is happening at that moment. We will have an attraction for remaining silent, and a tendency to adopt a calm, passive and silent form of prayer; we will put the Bible aside and wish to remain in the Presence of the Lord who is there. All of this is normal and it is often called *mental prayer*. It is necessary to be conscious of the fact that we are then engaged in *mental prayer*. If we have planned to engage in *mental prayer* for a certain time after *lectio*, we should do this, and on a regular basis. If we have not, we should stop the *lectio* after a maximum of 75 minutes. Indeed, we should be careful that this 'new form of prayer' does not become self-seeking, inspired by an egotistical desire to discuss the light we received.

When we read two texts, and find two passages that touch us, their content may seem general at first. It appears to be a general indication and advice concerning our life, but this is insufficient; we need something precise which touches our will and touches us today. The light comes through one or another word. Grasping the word, that is the first step; but this does not mean that the process of *lectio* is completed. We risk, at that moment, to interpret this non-specific light by ourselves, either in a general way or by giving it the sense we would like it to have. We must go back and insist again. Of course, from this point on we insist only on two precise and materially limited parts of the texts. Our reading will therefore be restricted to these verses - given that they now have only a single meaning. We see the light become more precise and more intense; it is more incarnate in us and speaks to us today. It touches our will and consequently our freedom, calling for a particular action. The action the Lord asks of us may be, for example, an act of detachment, an act of confidence. Simply pondering over the same light, with insistence, allows the message it contains to become more precise, clearer, more distinct and defined. We should therefore never hesitate to insist on the same words received on a given day: this will only make them become more incisive and efficient. If we dwell only on general, vague and inefficient aspects... they will not give us life.

Temptations to flight

Several temptations to flight present themselves and may become overwhelming at this moment, but we need to learn how to overcome them. *Lectio* is really the perfect ascetical exercise. Someone asked St Anthony the Great: What is the most difficult aspect in monastic life? He replied, saying "Scripture" (in the sense of 'bearing Scripture, suffering its weight of purifying and transforming light'). One must make an effort to remain seated. The Lord said the same to the monk Arseneus: "Stay seated, and don't move!" That is the effort; staying under the radiation of the Scriptures, of Christ speaking to us.

Here we find a list of the most common temptations:

- One temptation consists of only unveiling or exposing a part of our being to Christ. This attitude obviously lacks purity.

- Another, more superficial one, is to want to do something else that could really be done at another moment. The idea of writing a letter or doing other business will appear to dissuade us from exposing ourselves to the light of Christ. And the demon and we, in our most obscure parts, are repugnant to this light. This therefore is the effort that needs to be made; persevere and push forward to enter into the narrow path leading to liberation and true change.

- One might also say: "I know this text" and consequently be bored, *a priori*, even before reading it. Even though I assume I know the text I need to make an act of faith that this is the word of God and that he speaks to me today in a new way.

- We might be tempted to read notes and commentaries. It is certainly necessary to understand the literal meaning of the text, but the study of the text and the reading of commentaries should be kept for another moment. This is necessary but with detachment from the present process. It nurtures faith in general but it is not the same as *lectio*.

- We can also be tempted to take a look at what follows or precedes our present text. It is necessary to be prudent when doing this. There is a risk of digressing from a legitimate search for information, in order to understand the text and situate it, to squandering time and straying away from the goal of *lectio*. The boundary here is very thin and one must be aware, precisely because the big peril in *lectio* is that it may turn into textual analysis. We may receive light in this way too, but it no longer has anything to do with a word the Living Christ may speak to us through his Spirit.

Indeed, the process of *lectio* consists neither in studying nor analysing a text, it consists in listening and being receptive to the word.

Insistence and perseverance purify the heart

One cannot insist enough on this kind of perseverance, this stubbornness in asking the Lord what he wants of us today. The first request will always remain the key to *lectio*, its basis, its difficulty and its battleground. In fact, we should not talk about 'the first request' but about the *quality* of the first request'. We need to be able to implore the Lord with insistence. One may even imagine that by insisting like children do to get a piece of chocolate cake, we plague the good Lord until finally, tired and bothered by the clamour, he deigns to stoop down from the height of his glorious throne and give us a word. God does not find this insistence, this stubbornness irritating, because it achieves something crucial: it purifies our hearts. This happens precisely because we are pushed in this way to collect all the dissipated energies of our heart, and to direct them towards God. Finally, our prayer comes from all the cells of our being, through the pores of our body that implore the mercy of the Lord just like the poor blind man on the roadside who begged the Lord to heal him, believing that he would answer his prayer. The action of insisting and imploring frees our hearts from everything that encumbers them. Our heart is like a lounge where all the seats are occupied when Christ enters. No one gets up to leave even though we invite him in! The people sitting there are our worries and attachments, the multitude of objects that encumber our heart and prevent it from welcoming the Lord.

Keeping a written account

It is good to keep a written account of *lectio*. But we should not be in a hurry to write things down. That is not our aim. However, when two sentences or words are recognised as coming together, we may begin to write. These are the words we put to paper, precisely because they are the cornerstone and the vivifying sap, the light of all that may be written. Next, we can prolong this thought to some extent, developing it but without moving away from it, because otherwise we get caught up in human rambling; and the worst would be for us to believe that our own rambling words are inspired! Writing aims at crystallising thought, the light received, at giving it an intelligible form, helping the intellect and the body to realise what has been received. Writing also permits fixing thought. The written account becomes an objective witness, a mirror that lets us see ourselves more clearly. Later on, this will let us trace God's action, the thread of his grace and his direction. It is to be noted that, through our spiritual life, thanks to *lectio*, we move towards a progressive transformation of our being, it is conformed to Christ who is God; it is deified. God is simple (in his essence he is not composed, he is one). We are therefore constantly going toward a greater unity and simplicity. St Augustine was to say that the Scriptures speak of only one thing from the beginning to the end: "Love" (and God is Love)! For those who are not initiated, St Augustine's remark seems strange because apparently we find many things other than love in the Holy Scriptures, and especially in the Old Testament. However, God's love underpins them all.

For most of us, writing and putting the light received down on paper will take some effort. This effort should not be evaded *a priori*. As we said above, writing is in a certain way the first incarnation of the word that God speaks to us. Putting it down on paper gives it a form, defines its outlines and thus helps us to become aware of this daily event, the living encounter, through *lectio* of our conscious intellect with the words of the risen Christ.

Finally, writing is necessary, but it may also lead to distraction, especially for certain people. It is an instrument that needs to be well used. The date and perhaps the liturgical circumstance should be noted; they will serve as markers later on. The written account of *lectio*, of God's action in us, of the love letters he sends to us each day, form our spiritual history. However, 'spiritual' does not mean 'abstract', on the contrary, this dimension of our life is more real than its outer dimension. In fact, an inner world is founded and slowly begins to dominate (through its importance and priority) our outer life, which is often distressingly superficial.

Lectio is an authentic exercise of love

"One day someone asked St John of the Cross how he enters into ecstasy, he answered that this was by relinquishing his own will and doing the will of God. Because ecstasy for a soul is nothing other than leaving itself behind and being raptured in God - and this is what the person who obeys him does, because he leaves himself behind as well as his own will and, having become lighter, he attaches himself to God (or 'sinks into God')." This shows us that *lectio* truly is an exercise of love, since it supposes that we abandon ourselves each day in a loving, resolute and authentic quest for the truth. *Lectio* awaits souls who love truth and are not afraid of it. It seeks generous and courageous souls, capable of questioning themselves every day before God, ready to be converted.

Lectio is a daily verification of this self-abandonment

Lectio is a great way for us to be assured that we are doing God's will. It is a way of verification, a test, a true and practical confirmation of our desire to love God; it tells us where we are in our love for God. Loving God is simply doing his will, and the quest for this will is at the heart of *lectio*.

The consolation we receive in *lectio*

Because *lectio* opens the door for us to a true encounter with the Lord and to tangible daily conversion, it is also a source of great consolation. But this consolation is an inherent aspect of *lectio* itself; it is not added on, optional, nor is it a kind of gift the Lord bestows on those he considers weak. St Paul talks about "the endurance, and the consolation of the Scriptures" (*Rm* 15:4), God's action in us, his light, which illumines our intellect and the true transformation of our will, is the very source of all consolation. Searching for God's will and accomplishing it, through his grace, brings us the purest and most lasting joy and consolation. The Prophet Jeremiah celebrates this when he says: "When I discovered your words, and I devoured them, your words were a joy to me, and made my heart rejoice" (*Jr* 15:16).

The desire to convert oneself - the heart of lectio

Let us begin this new paragraph by some quotations from the Encyclical letter of Pope John Paul II *Veritatis Splendor*. These texts indeed deal with the question of conscience and the borderline case of erroneous conscience. This does not lead us away from our subject, since our everyday life, closely looked at, is like a case of an erroneous conscience, and precisely because each day we need to convert ourselves and be illumined by Christ. We are coming out of the darkness and moving towards the light.

"Conscience, as the ultimate concrete judgement, compromises its dignity when it is *culpably erroneous*, that is to say, 'when man shows little concern for seeking what is true and good, and conscience gradually becomes almost blind from being accustomed to sin'. Jesus alludes to the danger of the conscience being deformed when he warns: 'The eye is the lamp of the body. So if your eye is sound, your whole body will be full of light; but if your eye is not sound, your whole body will be full of darkness. If then the light in you is darkness, how great is the darkness!'" (*Mt* 6:22-23).

"The words of Jesus just quoted also represent a call to *form our conscience*, to make it the object of a continuous conversion to what is true and to what is good. In the same vein, St Paul exhorts us not to be conformed to the mentality of this world, but to be transformed by the renewal of our mind (cf. *Rm* 12:2). It is the 'heart' converted to the Lord and to the love of what is good which is really the source of *true* judgments of conscience. Indeed, in order to 'prove what is the will of God, what is good and acceptable and perfect' (*Rm* 12:2), knowledge of God's law in general is certainly necessary, but it is not sufficient: what is essential is a sort of *'connaturality' between man and the true good*. Such a connaturality is rooted in and develops through the virtuous attitudes of the individual himself; prudence and the other cardinal virtues, and even before these the theological virtues of faith, hope and charity. This is the meaning of Jesus' saying: 'He who does what is true comes to the light'" (*Jn* 3:21).

This is where we must introduce the action of the Scriptures as the Word of God which enlightens and illumines the conscience! God's Word is the sacrament *par excellence* of His light. However, "...the less serious our conversion to God is, the less clear the Scriptures are to us." This is why the person who accomplishes and searches for the Truth comes to the light (cf. *Jn* 3:21), and the Scriptures enlighten him. The first movement in conversion is to seek Truth.

Each person's first duty is to seek out the Truth and then to conform his life to it. In fact, sin is not only non-conformity of our life with what we recognise as the truth, it is also and firstly the refusal to search for the truth. There is thus a constant advancement in this discovery of truth. It is a task that lasts an entire lifetime. The document of the Second Vatican council on Religious freedom (Dignitatis Humanae) brings this to light: "all men are bound to seek the truth, especially in what concerns God and His Church, and to embrace the truth they come to know, and to hold fast to it."

Digging deep

"Every one who comes to me, and hears my words, and puts them into practice, I will show you to whom he resembles; he is like a man who, building a house, dug, and **dug deep**, and laid a foundation upon the rock. A flood came, the stream broke forth against that house, but could not shake it, for it had been founded upon the rock. And he who hears and does not act, is like to a man who built a house on soil, without a foundation. The stream broke forth, and it immediately fell, and that house became a great ruin" (*Lk* 6:47-49). 'Listening to the words of Christ' and 'putting them into practice', that is '**digging deep**' and 'laying foundations'. The more we do *lectio*, the more we dig deep, going down into ourselves and allowing God to descend within us. In fact, we are the ones who let God descend - or not - into our depths. This depends on the quality of our listening. Digging deep means descending into ourselves, letting the light penetrate our dark regions, at our deepest roots and our shadows. This depends on whether we open our door to Him or not; our freedom decides this. Our will to descend and to dig deeply within ourselves, this costs us a lot, yet it depends on us and solely on us. Facing the light, letting ourselves be illuminated by the light from the Word of God, that is our own task. We must face the Word, confront it, swallow it and digest it. This requires that we love the Truth, with a resolute attitude and a lively spirituality, and the desire that the light may vanquish our shadows.

God's action in us does not take place on the surface. It is orientated toward the depths. This action infiltrates our deepest being and frees it, making it subtle and deifying it. This is why deep silent prayer, *mental prayer*, is founded on *lectio*; precisely because *lectio* opens up the way for God so that he may go ever deeper in us through *mental prayer*. The effort of *lectio* opens the door to the divine beam of contemplation during *mental prayer*. In an ordinary way, without this effort God does not permit himself to enter into us through his supernatural action (the 'special help' of Theresa of Jesus).

A brief guide

We can now give a short description of the steps to follow in the practice of lectio. There are 7 steps in all:

1. Sit down in a quiet and solitary place - in the morning if possible.

2. Ask the Holy Spirit for help in listening to the Lord.

3. Re-read the two texts until they reveal one single light for today.

4. Ask for the strength of the Holy Spirit in order to put the light received into practice.

5. Write down briefly the light received.

6. Put into practice the word received today.

7. Verify at the end of the day that we have incarnated the word, and give thanks to God for it.

Conclusion

This method brings a real excitement and a deep joy into daily life. Every morning we can look forward to something new that Jesus will tell us. We are no longer 'lonely' because the guide is here and he is truly accessible. The channel to reach him is now in our hands. Many people have discovered this way to have a daily and living contact with Jesus, a connection that really changes their lives and brings God's light into it.

The third petition of the Our Father says: "Thy will be done on earth as it is in heaven". Through the *Lectio*, having first access to the knowledge of the will of God (which is to 'see' Him at work like the Son does), we may then accomplish His will. "The Son is not able to do anything of himself, if he may not see the Father doing it; for whatever things He may do, these also the Son does in a like manner; for the Father loves the Son, and shows to him all things that He himself does" (*Jn* 5:19-20).

We may conclude with this prayer which sums up the centre of lectio divina.

"Answer the prayer of your People,
Lord, in your kindness:
give to each person the clear vision
of what he must do
and the strength to do it."
Amen.

Informative Catholic Reading

We hope that you have enjoyed reading this booklet.

If you would like to find out more about CTS booklets - we'll send you our free information pack and catalogue.

Please send us your details:

Name ....

Address ....

....

....

Postcode ....

Telephone...

Email ....

Send to: CTS, 40-46 Harleyford Road,
            Vauxhall, London
            SE11 5AY

Tel: 020 7640 0042
Fax: 020 7640 0046
Email: info@cts-online.org.uk